THE NEED TO KNOW LIBRARY™

EVERYTHING YOU NEED TO KNOW ABOUT FAKE NEWS AND PROPAGANDA

CAROL HAND

Rosen
YA™
New York

Published in 2018 by The Rosen Publishing Group, Inc.
29 East 21st Street, New York, NY 10010

Expert Reviewer: Megan Fromm, PhD

Library of Congress Cataloging-in-Publication Data

Names: Hand, Carol, 1945– , author.
Title: Everything you need to know about fake news and propaganda / Carol Hand.
Description: New York : Rosen Publishing, 2018. | Series: The need to know library | Includes bibliographical references and index. | Audience: Grades 7–12.
Identifiers: ISBN 9781508176640 (library bound) | ISBN 9781508176633 (pbk.) | ISBN 9781508176664 (6 pack)
Subjects: LCSH: Journalism—Political aspects—United States. | Journalism—Corrupt practices. | Mass media and public opinion—United States. | Communication in politics. | Propaganda.
Classification: LCC PN4888.P6 H36 2018 | DDC 302.230973—dc23

Manufactured in the United States of America

CONTENTS

INTRODUCTION

During the 2016 presidential campaign, Pizzagate was a fake story centering on Hillary Clinton, the Democratic candidate for president. Fake news sites spread a story that Clinton and John Podesta, her campaign chairman, were involved in sex crimes involving children. The story said they were using a Washington, DC, pizzeria, Comet Ping Pong, as their headquarters.

How did this bizarre story get started? How did it spread? Craig Silverman on Buzzfeed.com gave a brief timeline.

On October 30, 2016, the Twitter account of a David Goldberg sent a tweet. It said the New York Police Department (NYPD) was investigating a claim regarding some of Podesta's emails. The avatar used for the David Goldberg account was linked to a white supremacist website, Stormfront.org. The tweet included a Facebook comment from a woman who accused the Clintons of running "an international child enslavement and sex ring." The woman, allegedly from Missouri, could not be reached or identified. A few hours later, a message board, Godlike Productions, said the conspiracy was "about to be exposed." The next day, conspiracy theorist Sean Adl-Tabatabai wrote a post for his website, YourNewsWire.com. He said an FBI informant had confirmed the sex-ring claims.

The YourNewsWire story was picked up by right-wing and pro-Trump websites. Donald Trump, the

4

Comet Ping Pong, a pizzeria in Washington, DC, was the site of the 2016 election scandal known as Pizzagate. The scandal was completely based on fake news.

Republican candidate, was running against Hillary Clinton. Many sites copied the material directly from tweets and message boards. Others added new incorrect claims. SubjectPolitics.com ran a story with this headline: "IT'S OVER: NYPD Just Raided Hillary's Property! What They Found Will RUIN HER LIFE."

The fake story quickly generated 107,000 shares, reactions, and comments on SubjectPolitics and another 100,000 on Red State Watcher. True Pundit published the story and added new fake charges, claiming sources including the NYPD and Federal

Bureau of Investigation (FBI). They received 110,000 Facebook responses. Three days after his first tweet, "David Goldberg" tweeted again: "My source is right!" He cited the True Pundit story as proof.

Pizzagate was completely phony. No evidence and no credible sources supported it. Yet it persisted for weeks, even after the November 8 election. Many people believed it, and it had real-world consequences. It may have damaged Clinton's campaign. The pizzeria owner and his employees were harassed. Their business suffered. On December 4, a man from South Carolina entered the pizzeria to "self-investigate" Pizzagate. He fired his gun inside the restaurant. No one was injured, and he was arrested.

People from Donald Trump's campaign and transition team helped spread the fake news story. Lieutenant General Michael Flynn served briefly as Trump's national security advisor. Flynn retweeted several tweets related to Pizzagate. Flynn's son, Michael Flynn Jr. was appointed to Trump's transition team after the election. According to BBC News, Flynn Jr. tweeted after the shooting, "Until #Pizzagate proven to be false, it will remain a story." Flynn Jr. was fired from Trump's team.

In March 2017, Alex Jones, who was involved in spreading the Pizzagate story, retracted the story on air and apologized to the pizzeria owner for his part in it. Jones runs the site Infowars.com, which has pushed many conspiracy theories. The conservative site Rare reported Jones's apology, which he read aloud online. Rare suggested that Jones's apology was carefully worded to help him avoid prosecution.

CHAPTER ONE

DEFINING THE TERMS

Most people want to assume what they read in news outlets and on social media is true. They want to trust the news. This means they must first understand how truth can be distorted or changed. They must understand the vocabulary of fake news and propaganda.

FACTS, TRUTH, OR LIES?

Something is true if it is real—if there is evidence to support it and it can be verified. At one time, the word "fact" was simple. It was a statement of truth. The phrase "true fact" was redundant—a fact was true by definition. It was a piece of information that was correct and based in reality.

On January 22, 2017, journalist Chuck Todd, on NBC's *Meet the Press,* was assuming this standard definition of what a fact is. Donald Trump's press secretary Sean Spicer had made statements Todd described as falsehoods. Trump spokesperson

Kellyanne Conway drew criticism when she described falsehoods made by press secretary Sean Spicer as "alternative facts."

Kellyanne Conway objected to Todd's description. "You're saying it's a falsehood, and Sean Spicer … is giving alternative facts to that," Conway said. Todd responded, "… four of the five facts he uttered are not true. Alternative facts are not facts— they're falsehoods."

Is a falsehood the same as a lie? The Merriam-Webster dictionary defines a falsehood as "an untrue statement" or "an absence of truth or accuracy." But the dictionary's definition of a lie adds a significant factor: intent. A lie is defined as "an assertion of something known or believed by the speaker or writer to be untrue with intent to deceive." A person telling a falsehood be mistaken or misinformed or may have failed to check his facts. He may be guilty of carelessness or poor research. But someone telling a lie is deliberately deceiving the listener or reader. When Todd called Spicer's statements "falsehoods," he stopped short of accusing Spicer of deliberate deceit.

HOW TO DESCRIBE AN UNTRUTH

Journalists are careful about accusing public figures of outright lies. This opens them to charges of slander or libel. Slander involves spoken statements that are false and damaging to a person's reputation. Libel is the written publication of a false and damaging statement about a person. Journalists who make such statements may be sued. They must prove in court that their statements are correct. If the damaging statements are proven true, the person has *not* been slandered or libeled.

Other terms describe less-than-truthful statements. Misinformation is false or inaccurate information. Often, it is intended to deceive; that is, it is a lie. Disinformation is false information involving large-scale institutions, such as a country's military. For example, disinformation might be sent to news media by one country's officials to destabilize another country. The Russian government routinely uses disinformation as a political tool—continually repeating false stories through many media sources causes people to believe them. Russia even gives journalists presidential medals for their effective use of disinformation.

Misleading information may contain some true information that is incomplete or out of context, so its meaning is changed. It may be contained in a news report that contains otherwise accurate events. Or it may be included in a fake news story. Use of misleading information makes it more difficult for readers to distinguish truth from untruth. This makes it easier to

Europeans keep up with US news, including fake news. Here, demonstrators in Belgium protest Trump administration policies during the visit of Vice President Mike Pence to a European Union summit.

spread fake news. Clickbait is Internet content, such as a sensational headline, that tempts the reader to click on a link—for instance, a headline about an actress wearing a revealing dress to an awards ceremony or a politician's words taken out of context to make him or her look bad. The article may contain some true information. But the headline, and often the article itself, are misleading. Highly partisan political sites often use clickbait headlines.

EXTREME UNTRUTH: FAKE NEWS AND PROPAGANDA

Fake news is content that can be demonstrated to be false but is deliberately packaged to appear as real or true. It is meant to deceive the reader or listener. The amount of fake news during the 2016 election year reached such heights that the fact-checking site PolitiFact named fake news Lie of the Year. This annual award highlights a "misrepresentation that arguably beats all others in its impact or ridiculousness." But, PolitiFact said, there was "such a deep backlash against being truthful in political speech" that no one person or political claim stood out. Thus, they simply named fake news itself the winner.

MediaMatters says propaganda, like fake news, is misleading or highly biased information. It promotes a particular viewpoint. Propaganda, it says, differs from fake news in that it is meant to influence opinion. It is not always completely made-up and is usually, although not always, presented as legitimate news. HCC Libraries Online points out that propaganda is used both to build support for a cause and to demonize those who oppose it. But it is often fake news and designed to appear real but can be proven false. Mark E. Andersen, writing in Daily Kos, suggests: "Let's call fake news what it is: propaganda."

FAKE NEWS VERSUS GOOD JOURNALISM

A good journalist rejects false information and demands truth, verified by several credible sources. When covering a congressional committee meeting, a reporter would seek out members of congress who had attended the meeting. If several representatives, interviewed separately, gave the same account, the reporter would likely be satisfied that the story was true. If accounts differed, she would ask additional

The press surrounds Senator John McCain before a Senate policy meeting. Good reporters will obtain comments from multiple senators.

questions. She would try to discover why accounts differed and what the differences meant. For a scientific story, a reporter would seek out expert scientific sources. These scientists might work for a respected university or a government agency. He would interview several scientists, making sure their facts agreed, and if they did not, why that was so. If sources differed in their interpretation of facts, his report would include these differences and the reasons for them.

Nobody's perfect. Occasionally even the best, most respected journalists make mistakes. A journalist may lack all the facts, be misled by sources, or word a story poorly, so people misunderstand it. When this happens, trustworthy news sources acknowledge their mistakes. They publish a correction and apologize. Fake news sources do not do this. They purposely present wrong and misleading information, made-up stories, and outright lies as fact.

MYTHS AND FACTS

MYTH: Fake news hasn't changed much through history; there is just more of it.

FACT: Some historians say fake news that mimics real news and intends to deceive is a new form of fake news. It is especially damaging because it spreads rapidly online.

MYTH: The best way to discredit lies or fake news is to repeat them and describe why they are wrong; good fact-checking will overcome fake news.

FACT: Repeating a lie gives it more power. Fact-checking helps but is not enough. It is more effective to tell a new story, from a reputable source, that illustrates the truth about the situation.

MYTH: Fake news is news you disagree with.

FACT: The term "fake news" is used incorrectly by many people to discredit the press. The major function of the press is to report the news accurately and truthfully. This news is not fake, whether or not someone disagrees with it.

CHAPTER TWO

THE RISE OF FAKE NEWS

Some people seem proud of making up fake news. Paul Horner, speaking to the *Washington Post*, says, "I think Trump is in the White House because of me. His followers don't fact-check anything—they'll post everything, believe anything. His campaign manager posted my story about a protester getting paid $3,500 as fact. Like, I made that up. I posted a fake ad on Craigslist."

WHY PRODUCE FAKE NEWS

One reason to make up fake news is to influence politics. Michael Cernovich, a California lawyer who built the website Danger & Play, describes himself as "right of center politically." He became known for fake stories about Hillary Clinton. He wrote that Clinton has Parkinson's disease and that her "inner circle" is a sex cult. Such stories are easily disproven, but Cernovich told *60 Minutes* that he considers them "one hundred percent true." In one month in 2017, Cernovich reached eighty-three million Twitter followers.

Partisanship, such as that shown by Cernovich, is a major driver of fake news. Amanda Taub reports in The Upshot, a *New York Times* website, that partisanship now acts much like racism in our society. Most Americans are deeply biased in favor of one political party. People choose to read only sites that are biased toward their own beliefs. A Trump supporter is drawn toward stories that praise Trump. Someone who opposes Trump reads only stories that cover his failures or scandals. When people read news from only one side of a situation, they develop increasingly negative attitudes toward the other side that end up reinforcing their beliefs. This "confirmation bias" creates a climate that favors fake news.

Michael Cernovich is a member of the extreme alt-right. He is best known for his role in publicizing the Pizzagate scandal.

Also, there is big money in fake news. Each click of an ad on a fake news site makes money for the advertisers—and for the site's creator. Paul Horner publishes his fake news on Facebook. He claims to make $10,000 per month using the Google app AdSense. If someone wants to write and publish fake news, there is nothing to stop that person. Media design professor David Carroll explains, "Anybody can make a site and put ads on it. They can easily set up a business, create content, and once it is viral, it drives traffic to their site." Shortly after the 2016 election, many people accused Facebook and Google of influencing the election by promoting fake news. Facebook denied the charge. But according to Abby Ohlheiser, writing in the *Washington Post*, both companies announced they would "crack down on" fake news writers trying to make money from their ads.

JESTIN COLER, FAKE-NEWS GIANT

Jestin Coler, also known as Allen Montgomery, founded a company called Disinfomedia. The company owns several fake news sites and employs twenty to twenty-five writers. Three days before the election, Facebook ran a story with the headline "FBI Agent Suspected in Hillary Email Leaks Found Dead in Apparent Murder-Suicide." It claimed to be from a site called the Denver Guardian. It got 1.6 million views in ten days and was shared half a million times. The *Denver Post* ran an article debunking the story and the credibility of the Denver Guardian. The fake site is now shut down.

Coler's reasons for creating fake news seem to vary with each interview. Coler wrote a series of fake stories about an Ebola outbreak in Texas. He dubbed it the "Fearbola campaign." The stories were viewed between six and eight million times. According to Michael Radutsky, CBS *60 Minutes* producer, "He said he did it because it was like an addiction. The more hits he got, the more of a rush it was." Coler also admits he makes a lot of money.

When interviewed by Laura Sydell of National Public Radio, Coler said, "The whole idea from the start was to build a site that could kind of infiltrate … the alt-right, publish … fictional stories and then be able to publicly denounce those stories and point out the fact that they were fiction." Coler was amazed at how quickly his fake news spread—and was believed. A story published on his site, the National Report, said customers in Colorado marijuana shops

Jestin Coler, CEO of the website Disinfomedia, created the fake news sites National Report and Denver Guardian.

were buying marijuana with food stamps. A Colorado state representative proposed legislation to stop the (nonexistent) practice.

Coler says his writers have tried to write fake news for liberals, but "they just never take the bait." He also says he has spoken to the media about the dangers of fake news. But he uses his alias, Allen Montgomery, so media organizations do not connect him with the Dis-

OUTSOURCING FAKE NEWS

Macedonia is a small Balkan country just north of Greece. Teenagers in Veles, Macedonia, turned the 2016 US election into a money-making opportunity. Goran is a nineteen-year-old college student. He wrote fake pro-Trump news stories by copying and pasting stories from right-wing websites. He wrote catchy new titles and sold the "new" (fake) stories to Facebook. Then he sat back and waited for advertising clicks to bring in money. Goran made about $1,500 writing fake stories for one month. He had friends who made much more. BBC reporter Emma Jane Kirby asked Goran if he worried that his fake news influenced the American election. He laughed. "Teenagers in our city don't care how Americans vote," he said. "They are only satisfied that they make money and can buy expensive clothes and drinks!"

infomedia empire. Coler says he plans to get out of the fake news business. There will be plenty of people to take his place, though.

HOW FAKE NEWS HAPPENS

Jestin Coler says he first hooks people with a headline and the site's domain name. He says, "You need to have a fake news site that looks legitimate as can be." People only read the first couple of paragraphs, he says. So you make those sound legitimate, and "you can do whatever you want at the end of the story and make it ridiculous."

Sapna Maheshwari, in the *New York Times*, followed the rise of one fake news story. Eric Tucker of Austin, Texas, accidentally started this story on the night after the 2016 election. Tucker saw several buses in downtown Austin. He took a photo and tweeted: "Anti-Trump protesters in Austin today are not as organic as they seem. Here are the buses they came in." Some of Tucker's forty followers retweeted it. Then, it was posted to the pro-Trump community on the high-traffic internet site Reddit with the headline, "BREAKING: They found the buses! Dozens lined up just blocks away from the Austin protests!" Over the next few weeks, the tweet passed through several other conservative sites, including Free Republic, Gateway Pundit, and several Facebook pages. It was shared at least 16,000 times on Twitter and more than 350,000 times on Facebook.

Tucker assumed the Austin protest was staged, and protesters had arrived in the buses. He said, "I don't have time to fact-check everything that I put out there, especially when I don't think it's going out there for wide consumption." But Tucker was wrong. The buses had carried people to a convention for Tableau Software. On November 11, the company tried to stop the fake story. The fact-checking website Snopes.com debunked it. Tucker eventually tweeted that he might have been wrong. On November 12, he deleted his original tweet. He reposted an image of it, stamped with the word "FALSE."

The denials received much less attention than the original story. In a week, Tucker's "FALSE" tweet

Demonstrators at Texas State University in San Marcos, Texas, protest Donald Trump's presidential election victory. Many such protests were organic, not staged, as Eric Tucker tweeted.

received only twenty-nine retweets and twenty-seven likes. The Snopes article was shared about 5,800 times. This fake story makes several things clear. First, fact-checking helps. A phone call to the bus company would have uncovered the truth. Second, a small following does not mean that fake news will not spread. All it takes is one retweet or share. Once the fake story is out there, it spreads much faster and farther than the truth. This is nothing new. BBC News quotes Winston Churchill (although this cannot be attributed officially) as saying, "A lie gets halfway around the world before the truth has a chance to get its pants on."

CHAPTER THREE

HOW DO YOU KNOW WHAT'S FAKE?

O n April 1, or April Fool's Day, news outlets print or broadcast fake news stories as jokes. People who should know better sometimes fall for these stories. Everyone gets a good laugh. This tradition goes back many years and continues today. In 2017, news media released a story that Britain's Prince Harry had married his girlfriend, Meghan Markle, in a secret ceremony in Las Vegas. Another story said Amazon had released Alexa for pets (it orders sushi for cats and launches balls for dogs to chase). How do people know such stories are fake? They know because they are ridiculous, or at least highly unlikely, and because they are published on April 1.

But on the other 364 days, how do people identify fake news? As more fake news is published and mixed with real news, the task becomes more difficult.

SPOTTING FAKE NEWS

The International Federation of Library Associations (IFLA) stresses the importance of critical thinking for

It is unlikely that a member of the British royal family would elope to Las Vegas, so a news report that Meghan Markle and Prince Harry did so should raise doubts among readers.

every literate, educated person. They produced a poster titled "How to Spot Fake News." If people follow the eight steps on the poster, it will help ensure that what they read is real, not fake, news.

Eugene Kiely and Lori Robertson of FactCheck. org point out that social media spreads news very rapidly. Readers should be skeptical of viral stories and check them out before passing them on. They should delete fake stories. If enough people do this, it slows or stops their spread. It is often difficult to determine if a story is true. A story that reflects negatively upon an individual or group might not be completely false. Some may be distortions containing partial truths. Kiely and Robertson quote David Mikkelson, founder of the fact-checking site Snopes.com. Mikkelson says fake news is a subset of the larger bad news phenomenon. Bad news also includes "shoddy, unresearched, error-filled, and deliberately misleading reporting."

Perhaps the number-one rule for analyzing news is "consider the source." Where does the story come from? Who wrote it? Are the author and organization trustworthy? Many fake news websites try to look like real news sources. For example, the site with the URL cbsnews.com.co is not CBS News. The correct site is cbsnews.com. The ".co" after the ".com" is a tip-off that a site is fake. Fake sites usually do not look professional. Some sites say they are "fake" or "fantasy" sites and that they publish fiction or satire. Others do not. Some sites fail to

TRUSTWORTHY NEWS SITES

These news sources are generally acknowledged to be honest and trustworthy. They present news that is actually happening.

- Associated Press
- C-SPAN (Cable-Satellite Public Affairs Network)
- CNN (Cable News Network)
- PBS (Public Broadcasting Service)
- *The Economist*
- Reuters
- NPR (National Public Radio)
- BBC (British Broadcasting Corporation)
- *New York Times* (left leaning but factually correct)
- *Wall Street Journal* (right leaning but factually correct)

describe their mission or list their staff members and physical location. This may mean no such organization actually exists.

A lack of an author is a second red flag. A fake story titled "Pope Francis Shocks World, Endorses Donald Trump for President" had no byline—meaning no author was listed. If this happens, the author may be fake. One story had the headline "Obama Signs Executive Order Banning The Pledge Of Allegiance In Schools Nationwide." The author was listed as Jimmy Rustling, who claimed the title Dr. and several Pulitzer Prizes to his name. A quick Google search proves this name to be a false one.

Next, what does the story say? A shocking headline may attract readers, but the story may be much less shocking—or unrelated to the headline. Some people may believe the headline but not read the story. Who are the story's sources? Do the people or organizations exist? Did they make these statements? Are the statistics true? The Pledge of Allegiance story gave the number of an executive order that had nothing to do with the Pledge of Allegiance. Again, a Google search can answer these questions. Sometimes no sources exist. In a March 4, 2017, tweet, Donald Trump accused the Obama administration of having his "wires tapped" in his Trump Tower residence before the 2016 election. Various intelligence experts testified that there was no evidence for this. But the accusation stayed in the news for weeks.

A story's date matters, too. A true story can be misleading if it is old but repackaged as new. Kiely and Robertson point to a CNN story from August 2015 titled

"Ford shifts truck production from Mexico to Ohio." After the election, a fake website copied the story and changed the headline to read, "Since Donald Trump Won the Presidency... Ford Shifts Truck Production from Mexico to Ohio." Trump himself took credit for Ford's plans. But this decision was made more than a year before the election.

SATIRE AND BIASES

Determining which news sources are trustworthy can be tricky. Just because people trust a source does not make it trustworthy. For example, there is the problem of bias confirmation. Liberal or left-leaning people tend to trust liberal news sites. Conservative or right-leaning people trust conservative sites. The sites say what readers want to hear, but this is no guarantee the information is true.

The Daily Show with Trevor Noah on Comedy Central gives biting commentary on political events. Here, Trevor Noah and Roy Wood Jr. converse during their *Democalypse 2016* election night special.

Sometimes people mistake stories on satirical websites for true stories. Satire uses irony, sarcasm, exaggeration, or humor to ridicule people or situations. But sometimes readers don't get the joke. They accept a satirical article as true. The *Onion* is a well-known online satirical newspaper. People have believed a number of *Onion* articles. A 2000 article was titled "Harry Potter Books Spark Rise in Satanism Among Children." This fake article was quoted for years in chain emails and on sites such as WorldNetDaily (a website that promotes conspiracy theories).

ASK THE EXPERTS

Most people don't have time to do serious fact-checking. They stop after a quick Google search. But serious readers should consult fact-checking experts. Some of the most respected are FactCheck.org, Snopes.com, PolitiFact.com, and the *Washington Post* Fact Checker. These sites determine the sources of stories and check them for accuracy and potential bias. They are not foolproof. But if several fact-checking sites find a story credible (or false), readers can usually feel confident about their analysis.

But who checks the fact checkers? The best sites have usually been free of scandal and controversy. However, in 2016, the British newspaper *Daily Mail* attacked the honesty and reliability of Snopes.com. Their information was based on documents from the divorce of Snopes.com's founders. Kalev Leetaru, a *Forbes* reporter, tried to verify the *Daily Mail* story. At first, he considered the story fake news. It seemed

THE BEST FACT-CHECKING WEBSITES

The website "Media Bias/Fact Check" lists ten of the best fact-checking sites:

- PolitiFact.com: rates accuracy of claims by politicians
- FactCheck.org: aims to reduce deception and confusion in US politics
- OpenSecrets.org: tracks money sources of candidates and lobbying groups
- Snopes.com: assesses myths, rumors, urban legends, folklore, and misinformation
- The Sunlight Foundation: checks money's role in politics
- Poynter Institute: leader in journalism; all stories credible and evidence-based
- Flack Check: political literacy arm of FactCheck.com; highly credible
- TruthorFiction.com: assesses political rumors and hoaxes
- HoaxSlayer.com: assesses Internet rumors and hoaxes
- Fact Checker by the *Washington Post*: assesses news; left leaning

scandalous and was not picked up by other mainstream media. He tried to verify the story by contacting founder David Mikkelson. But Mikkelson refused to answer some questions because of a divorce agreement. Leetaru stressed that fact-checking sites must be open and transparent. He could not decide how true the *Daily Mail* story was. However, since its founding in 1994, Snopes has had a sterling record.

CHAPTER FOUR

US NEWS AND PROPAGANDA

Propaganda uses words, information, images, or a combination of the three to persuade people of a certain viewpoint. It is essential in advertising. Why buy a Ford instead of a Chevy? Or Crest instead of Colgate? The products of different brands are often not that different. Advertising convinces people that one is better than the other. Propaganda is used in public health. Ad campaigns urge people to get flu shots or vaccinate their children. Propaganda has been used to convince people of everything from the need for war to the benefits of recycling. Advertising is product-centric, while propaganda is focused on a cause.

CANDIDATES USE PROPAGANDA

All politicians want people to vote for them. Often, they exaggerate their abilities or oversell how much better they can make people's lives. Perhaps they describe only the benefits of their job-creation plan and ignore its possible downsides. Or they rail against the few immigrants who become criminals but ignore the

millions who became pro-
ductive citizens. They sell
themselves and their ideas
with propaganda.

According to Your
Dictionary, politicians use
many techniques to craft
how people see them.
One is the "just plain folks"
method. People think a
politician who is similar to
them will work for them.
Donald Trump, who has
always been rich, appeals
to coal miners or other
working-class people by
saying he understands
their problems. Senator
Bernie Sanders also uses

Senator Bernie Sanders, a 2016
Democratic presidential candidate,
relates to people by campaigning
on topics such as health care.

this technique. A variation of this approach is having
supporters make ads saying, "I support Candidate X
because..."

Donald Trump is a master of generating fear. He
makes people fear illegal immigrants by equating them
with drug dealers, criminals, and terrorists. CNN's Fareed
Zakaria describes how Trump has used "fear monger-
ing" to build support for a travel ban against Muslims and
a Mexican border wall. Another of Trump's methods is
having a good slogan. Slogans make people think they
are supporting a good cause. Trump's 2016 campaign
slogan Make America Great Again adorned millions of
hats, T-shirts, and posters. Slogans, promises, name-call-

ing, or anything repeated often enough becomes effective propaganda. During the 2016 campaign, Trump constantly repeated demeaning nicknames for his opponents, such as "Crooked Hillary" and "Lyin' Ted," for Ted Cruz.

These techniques work because they appeal to people's emotions. The emotions may be positive—as with the feel-good slogan Make America Great Again. Or they may be negative, such as the fear generated by the image of terrorists surging across our borders. Fear causes people to dehumanize others and see them as the enemy.

MEDIA USES PROPAGANDA

Many non-news sources use propaganda to promote a candidate or a point of view. Political action committees (PACs) and larger super PACs raise money to fund political campaigns. Almost by definition, these groups use propaganda. Their goal is to persuade people to vote for their candidate.

PAC television ads use several propaganda techniques. The bandwagon technique urges the viewer to join the crowd and be on the winning team. The glittering generalities approach associates the candidate with positive ideals, such as family, freedom, or democracy. In card stacking, the ad presents only positive (never negative) statistics that support a candidate or cause. In all cases, the viewer receives a biased picture of the candidate.

Historian Lawrence Davidson emphasizes that governments also use propaganda. They use censorship to suppress certain kinds of information. Davidson notes that some university professors are prevented from doing research when their conclusions might be unfavorable to US interests. He points to research into illegal settlement expansion in Israel and research by professors from "unfriendly" countries, such as Iran. When professors protest this limitation of research, the government retaliates. State legislatures have threatened to cut off funds to universities and colleges that allow protests. Davidson says most politicians in these cases show "a knee-jerk impulse…to shut down debate."

MEDIA SOURCES FROM LEFT TO RIGHT

In 2013, the Pew Research Center surveyed 10,013 adults to determine the effect of political polarization on how Americans get information. Liberals and conservatives depend on different news sources, with little overlap. Left-leaning readers ("consistent liberals") most preferred NPR, MSNBC, and the *New York Times.* This group was more likely to have several news sources. Right-leaning readers ("consistent conservatives") overwhelmingly preferred Fox News. People with mixed views depended on a larger mixture of sources. But these moderate groups have little effect on the political process. The polarized groups are most likely to vote, donate, and participate in politics.

PROPAGANDA AND HATE GROUPS

Hate groups often try to force people to choose a side by setting up an "us or them" mentality. They sometimes use conspiracy theories to justify their beliefs. In World War II, the Nazis used anti-Semitic campaigns against the Jews. Now, some groups use similar campaigns to generate fear against Muslims. Anti-Muslim hate groups began to increase in the United States after the terrorist attacks of 9/11. In 2015, the Southern Poverty Law Center (SPLC) listed thirty-four such U.S. groups. During the 2016 election campaign, this number increased to 101. These hate groups see Muslims

Anti-Islam propaganda has increased since the 2001 terrorist attack on New York's World Trade Center. Here, anti-Muslim graffiti defaces a mosque in Dearborn, Michigan, in January 2007.

as alien, violent, and dangerous to the United States. They expect Muslims to undermine democracy and replace it with Sharia law, the Muslim legal system.

The so-called alt-right, or white supremacist movement, also uses hate propaganda. This movement is not new, but it became much more vocal during the election. Alt-right groups have racist, sexist, anti-Muslim, and other bigoted goals. They oppose immigration because it lets nonwhite and non-Christian people into the country. They want to replace traditional conservatives, whom they consider weak. The leading website of the alt-right movement is Breitbart News. Its chairman, Steven Bannon, became Donald Trump's chief strategist.

The racist Ku Klux Klan was emboldened by Donald Trump's hateful rhetoric during the 2016 presidential campaign. Here, Klan members march in a 2016 white pride rally in Rome, Georgia.

HOW PROPAGANDA AFFECTS PEOPLE

Some Democratic leaders thought Democrats lost the 2016 election because of economic issues. They say people were reacting to a system that puts rich people first. "Some people think that the people who voted for Trump are racists and sexists and homophobes and deplorable folks," Bernie Sanders said. "I don't agree." But Mehdi Hasan, writing for the Intercept, cites studies showing that Trump's win was indeed at least partly a result of racism. He quotes Philip Klinkner, a political scientist, who says, "The evidence from the 2016 election is very clear that attitudes about blacks, immigrants, and Muslims were a key component of Trump's appeal." Although economics no doubt played a role, Hasan says Trump's use of racist propaganda won the election.

Propaganda appeals to people's emotions. This is more likely to make people act than an appeal to intellect or common sense. Whether this is good or bad depends on the emotion tapped and the resulting action. Convincing kids to eat their vegetables has a good outcome. Convincing them to eat candy will likely have an opposite effect—obesity and cavities.

In politics, things are more complicated. At best, propaganda oversimplifies people's views. At worst, it can supply inaccurate or false information. Because it is biased, propaganda polarizes the audience. This might cause people to vote for a person for the wrong reasons. The best way to overcome the ill effects of propaganda is to recognize it for what it is. The informed person seeks out sources that provide a complete picture.

CHAPTER FIVE

THE DANGERS OF FAKE SCIENCE

Scientists work to increase our knowledge of the natural world and understand how the world works. The information they collect through the scientific process is accurate and reliable. It conforms to what actually happens in the world. It can be reproduced. It is an objective kind of truth, which remains the same regardless of a person's belief or point of view.

Good scientists collect observations and design experiments carefully. They check their results. They collaborate and compare ideas. They publish so their results can be retested and verified. No wonder good scientists get angry when their work is called fake science, and horrified when fake science is published and passed off as real. Fake science has become a serious problem in the twenty-first century.

FAKE SCIENCE OR REAL SCIENCE?

Inaccurate science stories can result from poor reporting. Science journalist Alex Berezow says many journalists

Climate scientist Katharine Hayhoe discusses climate change on the South Lawn of the White House in October 2016.

are not trained in science. When asked to cover a complex science story, they may simply rewrite the organization's press release. The resulting story is public relations, not science-based journalism. Also, Berezow says, journalists tend to sensationalize science stories if they do not have a scientific background. They may use click-bait headlines and make exaggerated claims not justified by the research. They may include their own biases in the story.

Authors of fake science stories—often based on fake research, fake conclusions, or experiments or studies that never actually happened—do not discuss research methods or use scientific terminology (probably because they don't understand science). They make no distinction between established science and fringe ideas. They do not point out limitations of the research but instead make sweeping claims that cannot be justified.

Pseudoscience is not based on scientific methods or evidence. For example, fad diets and natural remedies are routinely advertised with claims that sound scientific but are not. Emily Willingham, writing for *Forbes*, lists red flags that can help identify pseudoscience claims. Willingham suggests asking these questions: Who benefits from selling this product? Does the article use emotional words or sci- entific-sounding jargon? Does it use testimonials, rather than evidence? A statement from "Jenny C." claiming, "I lost 100 pounds in 30 days drinking Dr. Jones's mira- cle diet shake" is not scientific evidence!

PSEUDOSCIENCE IN ADVERTISING

In 1969, the organization Sugar Information ran an ad campaign that claimed sugar could decrease appetite. Their ads gave diet suggestions such as, "Have a soft drink before your main meal." Or, "Snack on some candy about an hour before lunch." The ads ignored sugar's relationship to obesity. Advertisers haven't changed much, but consumers might be smarter. In 2015, a public outcry forced a group called the Global Energy Balance Network to shut down its website. The group promoted exercise, while downplaying sugar's role in obesity. In 2014, the group had received $1.5 million in donations from Coca-Cola.

Between 2008 and 2010, both New Balance and Reebok claimed that wearing their running shoes could tone specific sets of muscles. Investigations showed these claims were false. Campaign US reports New Balance settled a lawsuit for $2.3 million, but not before selling $250 million in shoes. According to Investopedia, Reebok had to refund more than $25 million to customers.

FAKE SCIENCE PUBLISHERS

Fake publishers are also on the rise. These unethical, predatory publishers will publish anything if they get paid for it. They have no interest in accurate, reliable science. An India-based organization, OMICS International, publishes large quantities of very low-quality papers. In 2016, Canadian journalist Bryson Masse decided to test OMICS's credibility as a science publisher. He produced a "research" paper mostly plagiarized from Aristotle. He changed enough words so plagiarism programs would not flag it. OMICS accepted the fake paper and tried to charge him for publishing it.

Jeffrey Beall, research librarian at the University of Colorado, Denver, was disgusted by "predatory open-access journals." He tried to expose these fake journals by publishing a blacklist.

Jeffrey Beall, an academic librarian at the University of Colorado, Denver (UCD), kept track of fake science websites from 2010 through 2016. His website listed thousands of open-access journals (those available online to the public) that took authors' money but did not provide typical publishing services, such as peer review, editing, and archiving. Peer review is essential in science publishing. Other scientists in the same field read and evaluate scientific articles. They catch errors, biases, imperfect experimental design, and other weaknesses. Beall's website shut down in 2017. But a scholarly services firm, Cabell's International, is now publishing a similar list.

VACCINES AND AUTISM

The claim that vaccinating children gives them autism began in 1998 with a paper by British doctor Andrew Wakefield and twelve other authors. The paper linked the rise in autism to the MMR (measles, mumps, rubella) vaccine. Scientific studies were conducted, and many scientists were quick to refute the paper's claims. Over the next several years, the study was exposed as a fraud. Ten of the thirteen authors of the paper renounced the study. The medical journal that published the study formally retracted it in 2010. The United Kingdom stripped Wakefield of his medical license. But some people still believe the story. Between 1998 and 2010, vaccination rates in the United Kingdom dropped, and measles outbreaks

(continued on the next page)

(continued from the previous page)

occurred. Similar effects have occurred in the United States. Why does this fake story persist? First, some people blame a vaccine ingredient called thimerosal. But this substance has no link with autism. Second, people fear autism. Its symptoms often start to appear at about the same time children receive vaccinations, so some parents assume a cause-effect relationship where none exists. Emotional antivaccine stories by high-profile media personalities have stoked this fear. Some people believe these emotional appeals over accurate, statistics-based medical reports. Fake-science websites (such as BodyEcology.com and NaturalNews.com) continue to promote the fake story.

CLIMATE CHANGE MEETS SCIENCE DENIAL

Climate change is perhaps the most important scientific story of our time. It is already having profound effects on people and ecosystems around the world. The data demonstrating climate change are overwhelming. Over 97 percent of scientists consider human activity the major driver of this change. Yet, many people still deny that climate change exists and that humans are causing it.

A 2017 story on Natural News, a leading fake science website, reads: "The NOAA simply fabricates temperature data wherever it wants, creating the false impression that global warming is backed by 'credible science.' In reality, climate change is the greatest scientific fraud ever committed in human history." The National Oceanographic and Atmospheric Administration (NOAA) is the U.S. government's primary climate research organization. It has a network of satellites, ocean research vessels, and climate stations around the world. It continuously collects vast amounts of data. Thousands of scientists carefully analyze these data. They develop reports, maps, and models on which we base our growing climate knowledge.

Climate change deniers reject even the combined scientific work of thousands of scientists around the world. They even reject the reports of the Intergovernmental Panel on Climate Change (IPCC). Why do people believe fake articles instead of this climate change evidence? Some people think deniers simply need more facts—that if they understood the science, they would accept climate change. But studies show that it is not about science. It is about political beliefs. In general, deniers are older, male, and conservative. Conservatives think international action on climate change threatens trade and industry.

Many climate change deniers are in positions of power. In 2016, the U.S Congress had 182 climate change deniers—144 in. the House and 38 in the Senate. Three-fourths of Americans accept climate change, but more than two-thirds of them were represented by climate change deniers. ThinkProgress reports various reasons given by climate change deniers: Missouri senator Roy Blunt says there is no "real science" behind climate change. Kansas representative Tim Huelscamp says climate change is "not settled science." Senator Jim Inhofe of Oklahoma says global warming is "the greatest hoax ever perpetrated on the American people." The election campaigns of most members of Congress who deny climate science are heavily funded by the fossil fuel

In 2017, activists rally outside the New York State Attorney General's office. The attorney general was investigating the claim that Exxon covered up its knowledge about climate change.

industry and other industries that contribute to climate change. For example, Senator Inhofe received more than $2 million from these industries in 2016.

Industry disinformation and propaganda have shaped the country's view of climate change. Climate change did not make headlines until 1988, when the IPCC was formed and NASA climate scientist James Hansen testified before Congress. But Exxon Mobil, the world's largest oil company, knew about climate change as early as 1977. They did climate research during the 1970s and 1980s. According to an investigation by Inside Climate Journalism (reported in The Guardian), all scientific papers published by ExxonMobil scientists agreed that humans were causing global warming. But in public, the company funded disinformation campaigns. Since 1998, they have given $31 million to people and organizations blocking solutions and manufacturing doubt about climate change. They pledged in 2007 to stop funding climate change denial groups. But they continue to fund climate change denying members of Congress.

There is no magic bullet for separating real science from fake science. The same rules apply as for all types of fake news. Intelligent science news consumers should read multiple sources and make sure all sources are real, credible scientists and journals. Readers should also check their biases, looking at scientific evidence rather than preconceived political beliefs.

CHAPTER SIX

SEEKING TRUTH IN A POST-TRUTH WORLD

Fake news was 2016's Lie of the Year. Oxford Dictionaries chose a closely related concept for their Word of the Year: "post-truth." Post-truth relates to the idea that "objective facts are less influential in shaping public opinion than appeals to emotion and personal belief." In short, facts don't matter. In the United States and the United Kingdom, use of the word increased 2,000 percent from 2015 through 2016. U.S. usage centered around the presidential campaign, particularly the statements of Donald Trump. Journalists were shocked at how frequently Trump lied. "We concede all politicians lie," said conservative columnist Jennifer Rubin. "Nevertheless, Trump is in a class by himself."

A poll showed that voters considered Trump more honest than Hillary Clinton by eight points. Yet, when the *Washington Post's* Fact Checker rated 168 claims made by the two candidates, Trump received fifty-nine "Four-Pinocchio" ratings (the most dishonest). Clinton received only seven. Her honesty rating was in the same range as those of former president Obama and Mitt Romney, the 2012 Republican presidential candidate. This suggests that many people cannot (or do not) distinguish between truth and lies.

SOCIAL MEDIA AND POST-TRUTH

As Katharine Viner stated in *The Guardian*, "In the digital age, it is easier than ever to publish false information, which is quickly shared and taken to be true." The problem, Viner says, is that no one can agree on which stories are true. People base truth not on facts, but on what they believe to be true.

Donald Trump, Republican presidential candidate, speaks at a Las Vegas campaign rally in December 2015.

More and more people consider social media their primary news source. According to the Pew Research Center, "Facebook is the obvious news powerhouse." About two-thirds of American adults use Facebook, and half of them use it for news—about 30 percent of the U.S. population. Ten percent get news from YouTube, and 8 percent from Twitter. Thus, nearly half the U.S. population obtains news from these three social media sites. Half of these share or repost news content, and nearly half discuss news events and issues. These numbers are expected to increase as their use on mobile devices grows.

Susan Glasser, editor of Politico, has mixed feelings about this trend. On one hand, she says, social media has resulted in reporting that is "faster, sharper, and far more sophisticated" than when she began her career in the 1990s. But, she admits, it is also "the most efficient distribution network for conspiracy theories, hatred, and outright falsehoods ever invented." Glasser thinks the most worrying thing from the 2016 election is that the facts simply did not matter to many news consumers. The public now has access to many more news sources than in the 1990s. But can they evaluate these sources well enough to identify the truthful ones?

A LITTLE HELP FROM RUSSIA

The 2016 election woke the public to another source of fake news and propaganda—the Russian propaganda system. In October 2016, CNN reported an announcement from the FBI. They said the Russian government had directed computer hacks targeting the Democratic Party and Hillary Clinton. The Russians released these hacked emails to WikiLeaks, a website that publishes secret, classified, and leaked information. In November, the CIA released new information. It suggested Russia's goal had been to hurt Hillary Clinton's chances of becoming president, help Donald Trump's chances, and generally destabilize the U.S. election. In addition to hacking, they found evidence that the Russian government was funding "troll farms" to spread fake news about Clinton.

Clint Watt and Andrew Weisburd, in *Politico Magazine*, analyzed the results of Russia's propaganda effort, with chilling conclusions. They say, "[Russia's] canny operatives didn't change votes; they won them, influencing voters to choose Russia's preferred outcome by pushing stolen information at just the right time—through slanted, or outright false stories on social media." Russia has developed its propaganda (and hacking) techniques over decades. They use these techniques in European countries including Britain, France, and the Netherlands—and now the United States.

Julian Assange founded WikiLeaks, a website that published hacked information damaging to the 2016 Democratic campaign.

HOW POST-TRUTH AFFECTS THE WORLD

A major problem in the post-truth world is already obvious: Fake news is accepted as real, and real news is dismissed as fake. In this situation, the legitimate media—newspaper, broadcast, and internet journalists—are both victims and offenders.

A MODEL FOR RETURNING TO TRUTH

The value of a free press was shown during the downfall of the USSR, or Soviet Union. The USSR began in 1922 when Russia annexed a number of smaller countries. It maintained power partly by muzzling the press. Journalist Gal Beckerman, writing in the *New York Times*, says, "...the Soviet Union was the twentieth century's greatest example of a regime that used propaganda and information to control and contain its citizens—seventy years of fake news!" Citizens were prosecuted for speaking the truth. Writers were tried and sent to prison camps.

A backlash against Soviet suppression of the truth began in the 1960s. Protesters formed an underground journal called *A Chronicle of Current Events*. It reported on violations of human and civil rights. Contributors wrote in a sparse, objective style. They remained fact based, without propaganda or fake news. The journal was passed secretly from hand to hand. Those with news to share gave a note to the person from whom they received their copy of the journal. According to Beckerman, the journal published sixty-five issues between 1968 and 1983. It described political trials and abuses—things Soviet citizens could not learn about otherwise. In 1989, the USSR broke apart. Resisters hoped this would lead to greater honesty and openness. But in Russia, this has not occurred. Russia's leader, Vladimir Putin, is suppressing speech and press, eliminating opponents, and returning Russia to the old Soviet model of control by force and propaganda. Their propaganda also helps destabilize foreign governments, including that of the United States.

Donald Trump's rise is partly responsible for the "bad press" received by journalists (although fake news existed long before this). Trump has disrespected and even threatened journalists. During his campaign, he constantly accused the news media of dishonesty and spreading "fake news." This continued after his inauguration. In a February 2017 press conference, he called CNN reporting "fake" and the *New York Times* "failing." He stated, "I've never seen more dishonest media than, frankly, the political media."

In 2017, US journalist Daniel Ralph Heyman was arrested as he tried to question US Health and Human Services secretary Tom Price.

The media themselves have contributed to post-truth. They were strongly criticized for their continuous coverage of Donald Trump during the 2016 campaign, which gave him free publicity. Smart City Memphis gave a particularly biting assessment. They said, "the gravest sin committed by the TV media…was the lazy journalism that turned the nightly news lineup into reality television." Rather than digging for actual news stories, they said, the media delivered panel discussions rehashing the day's events.

The rise of post-truth damages science as well as politics. A false climate story in the *Daily Mail*, written by David Rose in 2016, shows how fake science is influencing Congress. Rose cherry-picked climate data (he chose specific details and left out those that disagreed with his conclusions). His article suggested that climate warming results from natural weather conditions, not human activities. His fake story was picked up by the alt-right website, Breitbart.com. The Breitbart article was accepted as true and tweeted by the White House Science, Space, and Technology Committee.

The loser in both attacks on the media and poor media coverage is freedom of the press, a freedom guaranteed by the First Amendment. The public tends to believe what is repeated over and over. If they hear fake news, that becomes the standard.

Stories spread over social media with no fact-checking. And it is much easier to follow emotions than to check facts. Many people believe what they feel is true, whether it is or not. Katharine Viner of *The Guardian* sums up the result: "When 'facts don't work' and voters don't trust the media, everyone believes in their own 'truth'–and the results… can be devastating."

IS TRUTH DEAD?

So, is society stuck in a post-truth world? Tony Watkins, writing for the Lausanne Media Engagement Network, suggests ways to get back to the truth. First, "Commit to finding truth." This might be difficult. It requires fact-checking and questioning everything. It also includes paying for good journalism—subscribing to trustworthy, high-quality news sources. Second, "Commit to challenging untruth." This means not contributing to fake news by sharing it. It means challenging fake stories with the truth. And it means speaking truth to power—for example, calling out elected officials who lie or who accept fake news as true.

Some people think companies like Facebook and Google should be forced to identify fake news and prevent it from spreading. Danah Boyd, writing for Backchannel, points out several problems with this. First, no one agrees on the precise definition of fake news. Second, the problem of media manipulation changes over time. Senders find creative ways around blocked content. Also, fixes may limit freedoms in ways many people would disagree with. Finally, fixing Google or Facebook does not fix the underlying problem. Building an algorithm to block content will not control fake news—or society's hate and racism.

Eliot Higgins and his group, Bellingcat, investigate world events using "open-source investigation." They piece together online information that is available to anyone. They develop timelines and determine the truth of witness statements. Bellingcat investigated the deadly 2014 air crash of Flight MH17 in eastern Ukraine. By piecing together information, they proved that the Russian Ministry of Defense had lied about the date on which a missile launcher passed through a Ukrainian town. The missile launcher had shot down the airplane. Higgins says his company exerts "peaceful power" and the "power of truth." It will take many dedicated people like Eliot Higgins working for the truth to stem the current deluge of fake news and propaganda.

10 GREAT QUESTIONS TO ASK A FAKE NEWS EXPERT

1. What is fake news, and how does it differ from propaganda?
2. What are some characteristics of good journalism?
3. How and why does a fake news story get started?
4. What are the best ways to spot fake news?
5. How can we determine if a news source is credible?
6. Why are fact-checking sites important?
7. Why do people use propaganda, and how can it be detected?
8. What problems are caused by the spread of fake science?
9. What is "post-truth," and how is it related to social media?
10. How can we limit or stop the spread of fake news?

bias Prejudice in favor of, or against, a person, group, or thing, usually with an intent to be unfair; for example, racial bias.

conservative A person who dislikes change and accepts traditional values and attitudes in politics and social issues; also Republican or right wing.

conspiracy theory The idea that an event or set of circumstances can be explained as the result of a plot by a secret organization; used to explain political, social, or economic events.

credible Believable, convincing; for example, a climate scientist with thirty years' experience in climate research is a credible source for a story on climate change.

disinformation False or inaccurate information, usually related to large-scale institutions; for example, one country might release disinformation seeking to destabilize another country.

fake news A news story that can be demonstrated to be false but that is deliberately packaged to appear true; it is meant to deceive the reader or listener.

libel Written or oral statements about a person that are false or damaging to the person's reputation.

liberal A person with progressive political views, who is open to new ideas and attitudes and is willing to discard or rethink traditional values; also Democratic or left wing.

misinformation False or inaccurate information, usually intended to deceive the people receiving it.

partisanship Prejudice or bias in favor of a particular cause, usually a political party.

peer review Reading and evaluation of scientific articles by other scientists in the same field, to catch errors and biases and to produce a scientifically accurate, truthful paper.

post-truth The idea that objective facts are less influential in shaping public opinion than appeals to emotion and personal belief.

predatory publisher (predatory open-access publisher) Publishers that publish papers for a fee, without benefit of peer review, editing, and other services expected of publishers; results in the publication of inaccurate or fake scientific papers.

propaganda Information, ideas, or rumors deliberately spread widely to help or harm a person, group, movement, institution, or nation.

pseudoscience A set of beliefs and practices that are mistakenly accepted as science, even though they are not based on scientific methods or evidence.

satire Writing that uses irony, sarcasm, or humor to mock and imitate real-life people and events; meant to expose, ridicule, and criticize viewpoints.

slander Spoken statements about a person that are false and damaging to the person's reputation.

white supremacist A person who believes and promotes the idea that white people are superior to all other races and who believes white people should rule society.

Canadian Association of Journalists (CAJ)
PO Box 117, Station F
Toronto, ON M4Y 2L4 Canada
(647) 968-2393
Website: https://www.caj.ca
Facebook: @CdnAssocJournalists
Twitter: @CdnAssocJournalists
The CAJ is Canada's only national association for jour-
    nalists. It advocates for all journalists and journalism
    students across Canada.

Canadian Journalism Foundation (CJF)
595 Bay Street, Suite 401
Toronto, ON M5G 2C2 Canada
Website: http://cjf-fjc.ca
Facebook: @cjffjc
Twitter: @cjffjc
The CJF is a nonprofit organization that works to
    "preserve, provoke, and enhance excellence in jour-
    nalism." They promote open and honest dialogue to
    improve relations between the media and public and
    private organizations.

Investigative Reporters and Editors (IRE)
141 Neff Annex
Missouri School of Journalism
Columbia, MO 65211
(573) 882-2042
Website: http://www.ire.org

Facebook: @IRE.NICAR
Twitter: @IRE.NICAR
IRE is a nonprofit organization dedicated to developing
    excellence in investigative journalism.

National Association of Black Journalists (NABJ)
1100 Knight Hall, Suite 3100
College Park, MD 20742
(301) 405-0248
Website: http://www.nabj.org
Facebook: @NABJOfficial
Twitter: @nabj
The NABJ is an organization of journalists, students,
    and media professionals who work on behalf of
    black journalists around the world.

Poynter Institute for Media Studies
801 Third Street South
Saint Petersburg, FL 33701
(727) 821-9494
Website: http://www.poynter.org
Facebook: @Poynter
Twitter: @Poynter
Instagram: @poynter_institute
The Poynter Institute describes itself as a global leader
    in journalism. Its goal is to elevate journalism and
    thereby strengthen democracy.

Reporters Committee for Freedom of the Press (RCFP)
1156 15th Street NW, Suite 1250
Washington, DC 20005

(800) 336-4243
Website: http://www.rcfp.org
Facebook: @ReportersCommittee
Twitter: @ReportersCommittee
The Reporters Committee for Freedom of the Press is a
    nonprofit association dedicated to helping journal-
    ists. They protect First Amendment rights and provide
    resources that help journalists collect and publish
    news.

Society of Professional Journalists (SPJ)
Eugene S. Pulliam National Journalism Center
3909 North Meridian Street
Indianapolis, IN 46208
(317) 927-8000
Website: https://www.spj.org/index.asp
Facebook: @spjregion3
Twitter: @spj_tweets
Instagram: @spj_pics
The SPJ is a national journalism organization dedicated
    to encouraging the free practice of journalism with
    high ethical standards.

WEBSITES

Because of the changing nature of internet links, Rosen
Publishing has developed an online list of websites
related to the subject of this book. This site is updated
regularly. Please use this link to access the list:
http://www.rosenlinks.com/NTKL/Fake

Belcher, Jason. *Fake News: The Fall of Critical Thinking and the Rise of Selfie Propaganda.* Amazon Digital Services, LLC, 2017.

Carey, Kelly. *Fake News: How Propaganda Influenced the 2016 Election, A Historical Comparison to 1930s Germany.* Marzenhale Publishing and Amazon Digital Services, LLC, 2017.

Fromm, Megan, Homer L. Hall, and Aaron Manfull. *Student Journalism & Media Literacy* (Book 1, Student Journalism & Media Literacy). New York, NY: Rosen Young Adult, 2015.

Gorman, Sara, and Jack M. Gorman. *Denying to the Grave: Why We Ignore the Facts That Will Save Us.* Oxford, England, UK: Oxford University Press, 1 Edition, 2016.

Harrington, Walt. *Artful Journalism: Essays in the Craft and Magic of True Storytelling. The Sager Group LLC, 2015.*

Levinson, Paul. *Fake News in Real Context.* Connected Editions, Incorporated, 2017.

Murphy, Danny. *Fake News Review, Spring 2017: Real news about fake news! Fake news about fake news!* Amazon Digital Services, LLC, 2017.

New York Times. *Fake News: Read All About It!* Kindle Edition. New York, NY: The New York Times Company, 2017.

Stovall, James. *Writing Like a Journalist* (Tennessee Journalism Series). Maryville, TN: First Inning Press, or Amazon Digital Services, LLC, 2013.

Andersen, Mark E. "Let's call fake news what it really is: propaganda." Daily Kos, January 8, 2017. http://www.dailykos.com/story/2017/1/8/1616368/-Let-s-call-fake-news-what-it-really-is-propaganda.

Anderson, Monica, and Andrea Caumont. "How social media is reshaping news." Pew Research Center, September 24, 2014. http://www.pewresearch.org/fact-tank/2014/09/24/how-social-media-is-reshaping-news/.

BBC News. "How do fake news sites make money?" BBC News Video, February 9, 2017. http://www.bbc.com/news/business-38919403.

BBC Trending. "The rise and rise of fake news." BBC News, November 6, 2016. http://www.bbc.com/news/blogs-trending-37846860.

Berezow, Alex. "How to Spot a Fake Science News Story." The American Council on Science and Health, January 31, 2017. http://acsh.org/news/2017/01/30./how-spot-fake-science-news-story-10794.

Boyd, Danah. "Google and Facebook Can't Just Make Fake News Disappear." BackChannel, March 27, 2017. https://backchannel.com/google-and-facebook-cant-just-make-fake-news-disappear-48f4b4e5fbe8.

Diamond, Jeremy. "Russian hacking and the 2016 election: What you need to know." CNN, December 16, 2016. http://www.cnn.com/2016/12/12/politics/russian-hack-donald-trump-2016-election/index.html.

Glasser, Susan B. "Covering Politics in a Post-Truth America." Politico Magazine, December 13, 2016. http://www.politico.com/magazine/story/2016/12 /journalism-post-truth-trump-2016-election-politics -susan-glasser-214523.

Higgins, Eliot. "Finding truth in a post-truth world." TedX-Amsterdam (video), 2017. http://tedx.amsterdam /talks/finding-truth-post-truth-world-elliot-higgins -tedxamsterdam.

Holan, Angie Drobnic. "2016 Lie of the Year: Fake news." PolitiFact, December 13, 2016. http://www. politifact.com/truth-o-meter/article/2016 /dec/13/2016-lie-year-fake-news.

International Federation of Library Associations. "How to Spot Fake News." March 28, 2017. https://www. ifla.org/publications/node/11174.

Maheshwari, Sapna. "How Fake News Goes Viral: A Case Study." New York Times, November 20, 2016. https://www.nytimes.com/2016/11/20/business /media/how-fake-news-spreads.html.

Smart City Memphis. "News Media: Finding Balance in a Post-Truth World." Smart City Memphis, November 28, 2016. http://www.smartcitymemphis .com/2016/11/news-media-seek-balance-in-post -truth-world.

Viner, Katharine. "How technology disrupted the truth." The Guardian, July 12, 2016. https:// www.theguardian.com/media/2016/jul/12/how -technology-disrupted-the-truth.

ABOUT THE AUTHOR

Carol Hand has a PhD in zoology with a specialization in ecology and environmental problems. She has taught college, worked for standardized testing companies, developed multimedia science and technology curricula, and written many books for young people, most on science and technology. As a scientist, she understands the need for factual information and the truth in all aspects of life.

ABOUT THE EXPERT REVIEWER

Megan Fromm, PhD, is an assistant professor at Colorado Mesa University and faculty for the Salzburg Academy on Media & Global Change, a summer study abroad program. She is also the educational initiatives director for the Journalism Education Association.

Fromm received her doctorate in 2010 from the Philip Merrill College of Journalism at the University of Maryland. Her dissertation analyzed how news media frame student First Amendment court cases, particularly those involving freedom of speech and press. Her work and teaching centers on media education, scholastic journalism, media literacy, and media and democracy. She has also worked as a journalist and high school journalism teacher and regularly teaches at journalism education workshops around the country.

As a working journalist, Fromm won numerous awards, including the Society of Professional Journalists Sunshine Award and the Colorado Friend of the First Amendment Award. Her first coauthored textbook, *Student Journalism and Media Literacy*, was released in November 2014. Fromm has recently authored texts on media literacy pedagogy and social media and youth empowerment. She also writes for PBS's MediaShift website EducationShift on topics such as media and journalism education.

PHOTO CREDITS

LORD MUMFORD'S MINX

Debbie Raleigh

Zebra Books
Kensington Publishing Corp.

http://www.zebrabooks.com

ZEBRA BOOKS are published by

Kensington Publishing Corp.
850 Third Avenue
New York, NY 10022

Zebra and the Z logo Reg. U.S. Pat. & TM Off.

First Printing: August, 2000
10 9 8 7 6 5 4 3 2 1

Printed in the United States of America

One

Standing in the center of the tidy office, Miss Cassandra Stanholte glared at the small, insipid Man of Business currently cowering behind the large desk.

"What do you mean there is nothing to be done?" she demanded, her tone as commanding as her expression. "Surely you do not expect me to hand over a sizable fortune, not to mention an estate that has been in my family for five generations, to some stranger who claims to have been married to my long-lost uncle?"

Running a nervous hand over his rapidly thinning hair, Mr. Albert Carson regarded the unexpected intruder in a wary manner. Although the young maiden appeared remarkably harmless with her demure gray gown and her golden hair tugged into a haphazard knot, he was not a bit comforted. Indeed, he was uncannily disturbed by the flashing silver eyes and stubborn jut of the softly rounded chin.

"Please, Miss Stanholte, I am suggesting nothing of the kind," he retorted in what he hoped was a soothing manner, "but you must understand that I am in a very . . . delicate situation."

"And what about my position? I assure you that it is untenable."

"It is not that I do not sympathize, but as you know, Lady Stanholte has provided a certificate of marriage to your uncle as well as a birth certificate for their child. She has also provided proof of his death in India last year. Clearly, we must at least investigate her claim that her son is legal heir to the Stanholte title."

Cassie bit back a delightfully rude comment. Although Mr. Carson was no doubt doing his best, she was in no mood to listen to his evasive explanations. In the past fortnight she had endured a horde of strangers invading her home, a near revolt by her tenants, the unpleasant gossip of her neighbors and a ghastly drive from Devonshire to London. She wanted a firm promise that the odious mess would be put to a swift end. Instead it appeared that she might lose everything while this timid man fussed over false certificates and the clever lies of an obvious charlatan. Really, it was more than any woman should have to bear.

"Mr. Carson." She moved forward to place her hands on the wide desk. "My uncle disappeared on a trip to the Continent thirty years ago. After his disappearance, my grandfather spent the next ten years and a vast sum of money searching for his whereabouts. Nothing was ever found. Not a trace that he was still alive."

"Yes, I recall my father speaking of the incident. Quite tragic."

She ignored his sympathetic words. "Naturally, the estate reverted to my father, and on my parents' death, to me. Now, do you not find it in the least odd that if my uncle were indeed alive he never made any attempt to contact the family, if only to ensure that he maintained control of his rightful inheritance?"

"Oh, yes, decidedly odd." Albert cleared his throat in an uneasy manner.

"Then why haven't you notified the authorities and had this . . . woman taken from my home?"

"As I have said, Miss Stanholte, proper procedures must be followed."

The devil with proper procedures, Cassie inwardly fumed, straightening with an angry motion.

"This is absurd, Mr. Carson. Any woman could claim to have married my uncle in the past thirty years. Indeed, for all I know, I might have a dozen aunts waiting to show up on my doorstep with heirs to the Stanholte estate."

"Really, Miss Stanholte, I believe you are exaggerating the situation," Albert protested, his tone flustered.

"Am I?" Cassie arched a golden brow. "It appears to me that all a person needs are a few well-contrived lies and a marriage certificate to acquire the title of their choice."

"I assure you that I am doing everything possible to discover the veracity of this claim."

"But how can you?" she demanded, her silver eyes flashing. "According to the supposed Lady Stanholte, my uncle died after conveniently leaving her a son and a deathbed wish to have him properly raised at the family estate. He obviously is incapable of verifying or denying any such marriage. Unless, of course, you propose to dig him up."

"Yes . . . well . . ." Clearly unhinged by the upheaval in his staunchly predictable life, Albert fussed with the cravat that appeared to be choking him.

"There are a number of inquiries I intend to make before anything is settled. Indeed, I have already sent correspondence to several acquaintances in India. We shall no doubt get to the truth of the matter in time."

Cassie was not appeased. It was all well and good for this man to speak of some eventual resolution of her predicament. His household had not been thrown into disarray and his servants on the point of walking out.

"I will not allow that encroacher to remain in my house while you dither over the finer points of the law," she retorted in sharp tones.

Albert lifted his hands in a helpless motion. "I am sorry, Miss Stanholte, but there is really nothing I can do."

"Then clearly I shall have to take matters into my own hands," Cassie announced, her delicate features set in lines of determination.

"Miss Stanholte, I would sternly advise against any hasty actions. This is a situation that calls for—"

"I know precisely what the situation calls for, Mr. Carson," she interrupted with a toss of her head.

Clearly sensing that Cassie was more than capable of plunging herself into disaster for the sake of family pride, Albert abruptly rose to his feet.

"You are understandably distraught, Miss Stanholte. I would suggest that you stay in London for a few days, perhaps enjoy a few of the entertainments, and then we will discuss this situation again."

Gray eyes flashed with a dangerous fire at the patronizing tone. "I have no desire to enjoy the local entertainment. All I want is that woman out of my house."